Seth Green

Home Fishing and Home Waters

A Practical Treatise on Fish Culture

Seth Green

Home Fishing and Home Waters
A Practical Treatise on Fish Culture

ISBN/EAN: 9783337139322

Printed in Europe, USA, Canada, Australia, Japan

Cover: Foto ©Andreas Hilbeck / pixelio.de

More available books at **www.hansebooks.com**

HOME FISHING

AND HOME WATERS.

A Practical Treatise on Fish Culture,

THE UTILIZATION OF FARM STREAMS.—THE MANAGEMENT OF FISH

IN THE ARTIFICIAL POND.—THE TRANSPORTATION OF

EGGS AND FRY, WITH OBSERVATIONS ON

COMMON FISH AND THE METHODS

OF CAPTURING THEM.

By SETH GREEN.

NEW YORK:

O. JUDD CO., DAVID W. JUDD, Pres't.

751 BROADWAY.

1888.

TABLE OF CONTENTS.

INTRODUCTION.

In the issue of this book the publishers of the *American Agriculturist* enable the public to secure a valuable work on the culture, treatment and habits of fish, from the pen of an accomplished experimentalist, who is amply provided with the experience and knowledge necessary to the task. Mr. Seth Green's name is of more than national fame ; his keen observation, his prolonged familiarity with all that pertains to the finny tribe, particularly in the inland waters of the United States and Canada, his thorough scientific equipment and his practical enthusiasm, give to his writings a character and authority, possessed by no one else, numerous and able as are his co-adjutors in the same field. Mr. Green has been engaged in practical fish culture for twenty-five years ; but fifty years ago he began to think upon the subject. The field grows larger and more expansive as the years roll by, and after a lifetime devoted to thought and action in this enterprise, he feels, as Newton did, that he merely stands upon the shore of the great and unexplored ocean of truth. That there is yet a wide area for discovery, he modestly observes, and

we may be sure he will not relax in the quest for
new results, so long as his wonderful energy and
vitality last. What the late Professor Spencer F.
Baird was to explorations in the waters of the
ocean, Mr. Green has been and is, to the activity
of research in the lakes and streams of our country.
The practical work of Pisciculture began in New York
in 1868, in the establishment of the State Hatchery at Caledonia, in Livingston County. From this
hatchery from one to two millions of speckled trout
have been annually distributed, and streams and pre-
serves in all parts of the country have been stocked
or replenished. There are many similar establish-
ments in various States, but those in New York and
New Jersey may justly claim pre-eminence. In
thirty-seven States and Territories Fish Commissions
have been organized, and a noble work has been
accomplished. The introduction of the German
carp, a fish in supply all the year round, except
during the period of spawning, is one of the most
valuable achievements of the period. The almost
incredible fecundity of fish is made to serve the
purpose of steady increase, and the young and exposed fish are protected from their natural enemies. A
codfish produces from one million to nine million
eggs; a salmon one thousand to the pound of
weight; a shad fifty thousand in all; a herring
twenty-five thousand; a trout from two hundred
to three thousand according to age and size. Under
ordinary circumstances, millions of these eggs cast
into unprotected waters, are unimpregnated, or are
lost or destroyed. It is the task of all fish cultur-
ists to prevent this waste in great part, and to pre-

serve these fish in accordance with the law of their being.

This volume includes directions for utilizing the streams and ponds that are to be found on farm lands. It describes the methods of artificial propagation, the care of eggs and fry, the process of hatching, and the modes of transportation to new waters. The maternal instincts of fish are delineated, and mention is made of the diseases of fish, their prevention and cure. The abnormal forms of some fish are noted in the strange "freaks" that are produced in the waters, and which mark the wonderful workings of nature, in disregard of its own fixed laws. Mr. Green points out a curious process of reasoning, as evinced in the action of fish, and shows that they are quite as alive to motives and results, as other classes of the "lower animals." The value of certain so called "common fish," is pointed out, and the methods of taking them, as well as the lordly bass, are described. The laws, relating to the protection of fish, are treated, and illegal and wanton methods of capture are condemned. The boys on the farm, and the men too, are brought within the range of discussion, and are taught how and when to angle, and cautioned against ill-advised destruction. Altogether the book will meet a want among anglers. It appeals as well to experienced old hands, as to neophytes in "the gentle craft." Izaak Walton writes : " This pleasant curiosity of fish and fishing, has been thought worthy the pens and practices of divers in other nations that have been reputed men of great learning and wisdom ;" and of Sir Henry Wotton, he says: " Angling was after tedious

study, a rest to his mind, a cheerer of his spirits, a
diverter of sadness, a calmer of unquiet thoughts, a
moderator of passions, a procurer of contentedness,"
an employment " that begets habits of peace and
patience in those that profess and practice it."

Governments, both in the States and in the Nation, have provided liberally for this new interest of
fish culture. The Chinese practiced the art many
centuries ago. The Romans understood and developed it. But in our own civilization, it fell into dis-
use practically, until about the middle of the last
century, when the work was revived and placed upon a somewhat intelligent footing. In furtherance
of these latter day methods, our Federal Govern-
ment has provided steamers and other vessels for the
prosecution of the fishing interests, both in the ocean
and in the interior waters. The electric light is used
in submarine exploration. Many of the railroads
have given willing assistance to the work of the
commissioners, in the distribution of eggs and fry.
Fish eggs to the number of many millions are ex-
ported annually and distributed in foreign waters.
These eggs are chiefly of the brook, California and
lake trout, of white fish and salmon. Bass, both of
the small and large-mouth variety, have been
sent abroad alive. So conspicuous has fish culture
become in this country, that Prof. Huxley, at the
International Fish Conference in London in 1883,
said : " No nation at the present time comprehended
the question of dealing with fish in so thorough, excellent and scientific a spirit as the United States."
Every year millions of fish are distributed in our
rivers and lakes. At the hatcheries, as many as

forty million white fish have been produced from the egg in a single year. A careful estimate of the annual catch of the rivers and lakes of the States, taking the tributaries on the Atlantic and Pacific coast line, and on the shores of the great lakes, with the minor streams that form the larger, is 184,783,050 pounds. To these must be added the commercial product of the sea; and the quantity altogether rises to enormous proportions. First in importance, fishing is the means of livelihood to thousands of people, and next it furnishes relaxation, amusement and healthful occupation to millions of men and boys all over the land; and we are pleased to note, to an increasing number of experimenters and devotees of the fairer sex.

The fish commissioners of the State of New York, in their last report, remark that the cost of hatching 100,000,000 of fish, including the expenditures for real estate, buildings, permanent improvements, labor etc., is $250,000. If of this number, one-fourth part or 25,000,000 live, the cost of each is one cent. At a fair valuation these fish are worth fifteen cents each. The investment, therefore returns 1500 per cent, or $3,750,000 for the $250,000, and the land and betterments remain. The commissioners in other States are able to make a similar exhibition of cost and product, and the people at large annually profit by this culture both at table and in pocket, and in the way of "sport." Laws are enacted for the preservation of fish, penalties are exacted for violation of these laws, and war is waged against illegalities in the shape of nets, lights, medicating waters, and the use of unusual and abnormal appliances.

The motive is in every way most worthy. The end is for the interest alike of the professional fisherman, the consumer and the sportsman. A humane consideration for the fish at a critical period of their existence has inspired these laws, and the people at large take a deep concern in their enforcement. The mere " pot hunter," and the wanton aspirant for a " big score," are under the ban of decent and right-thinking citizens. The instinct or appetite for destruction is corrected and men are learning to abandon abuses and subordinate their tastes and pleasures to a beneficent and well regulated system.

C. P. D.

CHAPTER I.

FARMERS AND FISH CULTURE.

No class of people should be more interested in fish culture than the farmers. Their homes are among the lakes and streams, and the lands which they cultivate border on them, and they, above all others, should be interested in keeping them stocked, so that when they wish a change of food from the regular farm diet, and think that change should be fish, they can get them for the taking, fresh from the waters in their immediate vicinity, without being obliged to send to the markets for them, with a little uncertainty (in such case) as to their being perfectly fresh. I do not wish to be understood as saying that fresh, wholesome fish cannot be obtained at our city markets, for they can many times be had, but in my opinion, the sooner fish are eaten after they are caught, the better food they are, and if you catch them yourself, there can be no doubt in your mind as to how long they have been caught.

I believe that fish should be eaten as often at least as once every week, and oftener would be better ; but perhaps I am a little enthusiastic on this point. There is scarcely a farm in New York State, and in many other sections of the United States and Canada as well, which has not a stream, lake or pond

within a radius of five miles, which is capable of supporting some kind of fish and furnishing fish food for
all the inhabitants in the neighborhood, provided
they are not allowed to be taken in any other way
than angling with hook and line, and are protected
during their spawning season. In one sense, these
bodies of water are natural fish farms, capable of
producing more food, acre for acre, than the land,
besides not requiring the attention and labor necessary to prepare the soil for a future crop.

After the seed is planted, nothing further is required than to reap what you have sown. Wind,
rain, hail storms, or cyclones do not damage them,
nor are the buds blighted by early frosts or the
fruit withered by late ones.

Farmers having a large spring or other water supply,
can have a fish pond of their own without great out-
lay, which in many cases can be utilized in winter by
cutting a supply of ice, which most farmers now consider a necessity.

After a pond has been built a year or two, it will
breed enough food to support a number of fish, and
it will not be necessary to feed them. The older
the pond the better, and the more fish it is capable
of supporting. If fish are put in a new pond, they
should be fed, as fish cannot live and thrive without
plenty of food, any more than the stock on your
farms.

In regard to the size to build your pond, the
quantity of water which is to supply it, should be
taken into consideration, and also the kind of fish to
be kept in it. For trout, it should not be built so large
but that it will get a complete change of water

every twenty-four or forty-eight hours. For bass or perch, if the water changes once a week it will answer. With carp, only enough water is required to keep up with the evaporation, and the warmer the water gets, the better and the faster the growth of the fish, provided they have plenty of food.

Many farms have soft, springy portions which cannot be used for the growing of crops, in which a fish pond could be constructed without great expense, and enough raised for family use. But in the taking of fish, whether it be from a natural body of water or from a private pond, you should regulate the killing of them the same as you would your fowls. Do not kill any more than you need at one time, for although you cannot see the fish to count them the same as you can your fowls, yet the fact remains that when one of each is killed, there remains one less fish or chicken for future dinners, as the case may be, and you should no more think of killing more fish than you would use, than you would chickens. I know, the temptation is too strong to resist, when fish are biting well, to stop taking them when you have enough for your own use ; but if you do take them, do not let them go to waste. You have plenty of neighbors who would be glad of them, and perhaps some day when your provisions happened to be low, you might go home and find that a neighbor who had not forgotten your kindness, had sent something in.

CHAPTER II.

THE WASTE OF SEEDS AND EGGS BY NATURE'S METHODS.

IT is somewhat singular to note the method with which nature has carried out her design in the apparent over-production of the millions of seeds of plants and trees, and the millions of eggs fish are made to produce. Many millions of each perish if left to themselves, leaving comparatively few to grow, and of these but a small percentage ever reach maturity.

How many have noticed, in the fall of the year, the countless numbers of seeds falling from the trees, and have seen them swept about by the winds, covered up by leaves, blown into the water; and the next year, out of the myriads that fell, but few hundreds ever raise their heads above the soil. Perhaps the spot in which they have been cast is unfavorable to their growth; the land may not be rich enough to properly nourish them; weeds may spring up and choke them, and there are numerous other causes, quite familiar why they will never survive. Only one out of many ever reaches full development, to reproduce its own kind. As with plants, so with fish. A wise Director has given them large quantities of eggs, knowing that with these, as with seeds, many are destined never to reach maturity, and for causes, though widely different in their nature, yet comparatively the same. When the eggs are first emitted from the female fish, the chances are more than even that they will not be vitalized by coming in contact with the living germs of the male fish, and in case they do not, they are worthless, and if not devoured by some other fish or insects, they soon decay and are lost to sight. If the egg has been properly vitalized, let us follow it, and see some of the numerous dangers which beset it, before it shall have changed its form into a fish. In the first place, all kinds of fish are fond of spawn as food, and consider it a great delicacy ; hence they are constantly on the look-out for the tempting morsel. A large number of water-bugs, reptiles, and many birds and quadrupeds also, look upon spawn as a desirable food, so that the eggs are in constant danger of being devoured by some one of their many voracious enemies.

Though the egg may be fortunate enough to escape destruction, as above described, "Dame Fortune" must smile on it to a still further extent. If the egg should happen to be carried along with the current, and get covered with the sediment which is constantly flowing in all streams, to a greater or less extent, it would soon die from suffocation. In order that it may hatch, it must lodge in some secluded nook, where it will constantly be agitated to a slight degree by the action of the water, or it must lie directly over where a spring bubbles up, and under these circumstances only, will the egg be liable to produce a fish. We will suppose the egg has escaped destruction, and the little prisoner has broken through the shell. With many kinds of fish, when the young fry first emerges from the egg, it is encumbered with a yolk sac, larger in bulk than all the rest of it put together; this sac extends from the gills to the vent, and as long as this remains, the little fish does not require food. The length of time the sac remains on the fry, varies with different kinds of fish. With the fall-spawning kinds of fresh water fish, as the brook trout, salmon trout, salmon, etc., it usually requires from thirty to forty-five days, before it is absorbed. With the fish which cast their spawn in the spring and summer, as the bass, shad, perch, etc., but a few days are required before they are relieved of nature's nursing bottle. One great reason why a larger percentage of the spawn and young fish of the spring spawners survive, is because it takes them such a short time to hatch and develop sufficiently to protect themselves from their enemies, by escaping and hiding. While the fall spawners, which are from sixty to one hundred days, and sometimes even longer in hatching, are much more liable to be destroyed. The difference in the time of hatching, depends upon the temperature of the water; the warmer it is, the sooner they hatch. With the spawn taken in the fall, each degree of warmth in the water hastens the hatching period five days, and each degree of cold retards it for the same length of time. While with the spring spawners, each degree of heat or cold, makes about one day's difference in hatching.

CHAPTER III.

THE ADVANTAGES OF FISH CULTURE.

IN the foregoing chapter I attempted to explain the dangers and the liability to destruction to which the eggs and young fry are exposed when left to develop by the natural course provided for them. I will now try to explain how the artificial propagation of fish overcomes the dangers which beset them, and protects and cares for the young fry, until they are, in a measure, capable of looking out for themselves, and how it increases the product over the natural method.

The fish culturist selects the ripe fish which are about to cast their spawn, and by handling them very carefully, extracts the spawn from the female, and vivifies it by placing it in contact with the living germs from the male fish. This, if done correctly, and if the parent fish are in the proper condition, should vitalize from ninety to one hundred per cent of the eggs taken. When I first began my labors in pisciculture, the best impregnation by artificial means then known, was twenty-five per cent. The practice then in vogue was, in taking the spawn by hand, to strip it into a pan about half full of water; but by a series of experiments and gradually reducing the quantity of water, I found that the highest results were attained by using very little water, or even none at all. This then was a great advance, and I have continued to employ this process in all my operations ever since.

After the spawn has been taken and vitalized as above described, it is allowed to stand in the pans for a certain length of time, usually from twenty to thirty minutes ; the eggs are then rinsed off and are placed in the hatching troughs or other hatching apparatus. Here they are allowed to remain until they hatch, which, as I have explained in the last chapter, varies in length of time with different varieties of fish, some requiring a longer and some a shorter period. When the eggs are in the hatching apparatus, they are directly under the fish culturist's eye. He watches over them daily with almost as much care as a mother does her child, to see that they are receiving the proper circulation which they must have in order to hatch, and although precautions are taken to exclude their enemies, they are liable to get among the spawn and destroy the eggs. In my early experience I noticed the eggs dying in certain parts of my hatching troughs, and also observed that some were missing. I was not long in discovering that rats were the cause of the trouble, and a few steel traps judiciously set, soon disposed of them. I mention this to show that enemies which we would least suspect, have to be discovered and guarded against. On one occasion I took the shells of three hundred eggs from the stomach of one rat. While the eggs are in the process of hatching, they must be looked over and examined every day, and if any dead ones are discovered, they must be immediately removed. The reason for this is that after an egg has been dead for a short time a fungus growth begins to encircle it, the feathery arms of which reach out from it, and coming in contact with the living eggs, deal death among them. Unless removed in time, one dead egg will be the means of destroying thousands of others. It must therefore be taken out before it has had time to develop this fungus growth.

Many people have doubtless had occasion to note how detrimental one decaying peach in a basket is to those which happen to lie in close proximity to it. Well, this is precisely the same effect the decaying egg has upon others, and it must for the same reason be removed. When the spawn has laid in the hatching apparatus the proper time for the eggs to hatch, the little fish which is plainly seen moving in the egg some time before it hatches, breaks through the shell, straightens itself out, and is a fish. They are then, in the case of most varieties of young fry, very helpless. The large yolk-sac which is attached to their bodies renders locomotion difficult, and unless protected, they would fall an easy prey to their enemies. The fish culturist looks after them until they are relieved of this encumbrance, or nearly so, and then they are in condition to strike out for themselves and fight the battle of life. True, many are liable to be destroyed even at this period. The same rule follows with fish as in human nature :—The big fish eat the little ones. But they have had a big lift on their journey in having been protected through their most helpless and exposed period.

CHAPTER IV.

THE MOTHERLY CARE OF SOME FISHES.

HAVING told my readers something about the beneficial results of fish culture, and how the fish culturist acts as a foster - mother to the young fry, I will mention a few fresh-water fishes that do not need the protection and care in handling their spawn, which is necessary with other kinds. Most notably among these are the Black Bass and Bull-head.   Nature seems to have endowed these fish with certain motherly instincts, which lead them to protect their spawn from their numerous enemies until it is hatched, and then look after the young fry until they have in a measure learned to take care of themselves.   All they need is the protection of the law to guard against their being caught, or disturbed while they are engaged in casting their spawn.   The black bass more particularly needs protection.   The bull-head has shown its ability to keep up with the fisherman, without any protection whatever.

The black bass in the northern part of the country, cast their spawn principally during the month of June.   They prepare their nests on a rocky bottom, and after the spawn has been cast and impregnated, the female stands guard over them during the hatching period, which is usually from five to

seven days, varying according to the temperature of
the water. After they are hatched, the young fry
are about as helpless as young robins ; hence the
mother stays with them until they have learned to
feed, and then the brood scatter, and the family ties
are severed forever. The black bass is a very plucky
and game fish, and when in charge of the little ones
is very ferocious, and will dart at all intruders who
venture near, and unless they make haste to get out
of the way, some one is very liable to get hurt.

The brook trout is considered a much more gentle
fish, lives in beautiful little streams, and is much
more handsome to look upon, but for all that, these
fish are cannibals in their nature, and would not
hesitate to devour their own spawn or young fry, if
they felt the need of them.

In all waters suitable for them, the black bass
increase very rapidly, forty or fifty mature fishes being sufficient to stock any waters in the course of a
few years. The reason of this is because of the protection given their young, as explained above.

The bull-head is a fish not to be despised. It is a
native of many of our rivers, lakes and ponds, and is
very prolific, one pair breeding about one thousand
fry. It is an excellent fish for the people, for the
reason that it is very plenty, and easy to catch.
They are caught principally in roily or muddy water,
for the reason that they depend upon their nose
to discover their food ; they follow the scent, the
same as a dog. Their method of breeding is as follows : after they mate, they dig a hole in the side
of a bank, and sometimes on the bottom, and then
excavate a sort of cave, about two feet across, and

seven or eight inches deep. After the spawn is deposited, the water is fanned with the tail and fins, and the dirt kept away from it. The eggs hatch in about five days, late in June, or early in July. When the fry are hatched, they lie around a few days, until they gain strength to follow their mother. The parent fish then cares for them, and teaches them to feed just as a hen does her chicks, until the little fish are about four weeks old. By that time they have learned to feed, and are able to take care of themselves. Bull-heads do not thrive well in small ponds, unless they are well fed and caught out. They are such prolific breeders that the pond rapidly fills with them, and they cannot get enough to eat. I have seen them in a pond containing an acre or two, where they were nearly all head, and in a starved condition, so that they never grew over seven or eight inches in length. They are unlike many other fish, and do not live on their young; consequently they starve where other fish would thrive—on the principle of the " survival of the fittest."

If the mother fish should be caught or killed, before the young are taught to feed, they would be almost sure to die. Fishermen sometimes find the holes which are occupied by the old fish and her brood, and both parents are speared ; in such cases, the young fry lie about the mouth of the hole and die. They rarely exceed a pound in weight in most waters, but there are varieties in some waters that I have known, where they sometimes grow to weigh two pounds. The bull-head is often confounded with the cat-fish, but it is a different fish. They are quite readily distinguished by their tails. The former has a square, or rounded tail, while the other has a forked tail. The cat-fish grows to enormous size. In the rivers of the South and West—it sometimes reaches one hundred pounds.

CHAPTER V.

THE SAFETY INSTINCT OF FISH.

WHEN a wise Creator filled the forests with game and the waters with fish, there is no doubt He foresaw that they were in time destined to disappear. With His far-seeing eye, He knew that the tillers of the soil would furnish a substitute for the game. He placed enough of the game within the reach of the pioneer, so that he could have fresh meat for himself and family until they could raise crops, cattle, sheep, and fowls, and it would then be unnecessary for them to depend upon the natives of the wild woods for subsistence. With fish the case was different; there was no substitute for them. It was inevitable that a lighter food would be necessary for the health of His people, and in consequence thereof, He gave each fish large quantities of eggs so they would not diminish; but it was in the order of things that not more than one egg in five hundred cast, would hatch naturally and grow to a size sufficient for table use.

He also foresaw that in time the earth's surface would be thickly populated, and that the food resources would be taxed to the utmost. Under this state of affairs the fish supply would be drawn upon to its fullest extent, and when nature's methods were found to be inadequate to supply the unnatural drain, the discovery of artificial fish culture would be brought to its relief. Without this, fish must have disappeared with the game.

The advance of civilization is fast driving the monarchs of the forest and prairie out of existence. The deer, the bear, and the buffalo are becoming scarce in their native haunts, and not many more generations will have passed, before our descendants will gaze in wonder at the stuffed specimens now preserved in our museums ; at the creatures which ages ago roamed wild and free over the very ground where large cities have sprung up and flourished.

Agriculture and fish culture should go hand in hand, and I am much gratified to see the interest which is displayed on the part of the farmers in the cultivation of fish.

The fish culturist in re-stocking depleted waters, has many things to contend against which can be avoided in dealing with stock on our farms. We cannot keep the fish separated. We oftentimes find that certain waters are adapted to the most choice varieties of fish, and in the same localities will be found some of their most deadly enemies.

If would be a fair comparison if the farmer should put a wolf in his sheep pasture. Now if the farmer found it necessary to do this, he would do as the fish culturist has to do, put in enough sheep so as to have some left, after the wolf had satisfied his voracious appetite.

It is astonishing to see how quickly young fish learn to distinguish their enemies. They show a great deal of shrewdness and cunning in escaping from them. In fact, it seems to be born in them, and it is undoubtedly that instinct of self-preservation with which every organism that possesses animal life seems to be endowed.

The home of nearly all kinds of young fish is near the shore, and if by chance, in search of food or otherwise, they should happen to get too far out, and an unforeseen enemy should suddenly make his appearance, they set their little propellers in rapid motion to reach the shallow water where the larger fish cannot go; and when a little fellow reaches the goal, if he is not too frightened, I have no doubt that he chuckles to himself to think how he has fooled his pursuer, or as I have seen them when they were so far out that they could not gain the shore, before they were overtaken and devoured, they will with a quick turn of the body suddenly dive into the mud on the bottom. On one occasion which came under my observation, a chub was making for a little trout, doubtless smacking his lips in anticipation of the tempting morsel, when suddenly the trout disappeared, leaving his chubship in mute astonishment as to what had become of his prey.

But all small fry are not so fortunate, and the pursuer often displays as much skill as the pursued. Few people know much about the great reasoning powers of fish, insects and dumb animals, and it is doubtful whether we shall ever understand the nature and extent of these senses.

CHAPTER VI.

HOW SPAWN IS TAKEN FROM FISH.

MANY people have the impression that the fish must be cut open in order to obtain its spawn, but such is not the case. When the spawn is taken from the female fish to be vitalized with the milt of the male, both parents must be alive and in a healthy condition, or else good results cannot be obtained.

On one occasion we took the spawn from a ripe female three hours after she was supposed to be dead, and impregnated it by using a live male. After the spawn had developed sufficiently to ascertain, fifteen per cent. were found impregnated, but it is doubtful if every spark of life had departed from the female, as the blood will often circulate long after a fish has ceased to show any signs of life.

After the fish are captured from the spawning races, into which they have run in anticipation of casting their spawn in the natural way, they are placed in a tub of water and the ripe females selected. Experience is about the only thing which will tell you with certainty when the female is in perfect condition for operating upon. The eggs must be perfectly mature, and ready to come from the fish, just as nature intended they should. If they are pressed from the fish prematurely, your efforts will be wasted, as such eggs cannot be fertilized. The ripe female, by an expert, can be told by the touch. When in perfect condition, the belly of the fish feels

soft and flabby, and if she were held up by the head
her spawn would settle downward, while with the
unripe female, the spawn remains stationary in
place, and feels to the touch hard and bunchy, like
shot.

When all is in readiness, the fish is taken by the
head with the right, and by the lower part of the
body with the left, hand, and held over the pan, with
the belly as near the bottom as possible. The fish
will struggle quite violently at first; it is many times
necessary to place it back in the tub for a moment
and commence again. When the fish gets quiet,
the right hand is gently slipped down from the upper
part of the body, and the forefinger used to press the
belly, the hold on the tail or lower part of the fish
being retained. If the fish is a large one, it is often
necessary for the operator to have an assistant to
hold its head, as it would be very difficult for one
person both to hold and take the eggs, without
injuring the fish.

If the fish are handled too roughly, the slime which
covers the bodies of the fish will be broken, and in
that case a fungus growth appears upon them, and
the result is almost invariably death. In some instances they may be cured by immersing them
several times in a strong salt water bath until they
turn over, and then placing them immediately in
fresh water; but this is rarely effectual. The pan may
be slightly elevated on one side by placing a small
block under it about an inch in thickness; this is so
that the spawn and milt will occupy less space. The
bottom of the pan should be moistened by dipping it
into water and immediately pouring it out. This is

all the water that should be used, aside from what would naturally drip from the fish.

The impregnation takes place instantaneously.

After the spawn and milt have been taken, they should be jostled about in the pan for a short time, so as to thoroughly mix. More water is then added: when the eggs adhere to each other and to the side of the pan. The spawn is then set in a hatching trough where the water is flowing ; in about twenty or thirty minutes it loosens up and separates. It should then be washed in several waters, and placed on the hatching trays.

CHAPTER VII.

THE REASONING POWER OF FISHES.

Few people know that fishes possess intelligence and reasoning power. In my long experience with fishes I have many times witnessed actions on their part, which could not have been performed if they had not possessed a certain amount of reasoning faculty, over and above what is commonly termed instinct, with which all animal life is endowed.

I will give a few observations which have caused me to believe that fishes can reason. In the winter of 1840 I hunted deer and fished for salmon trout in and around Bonaparte Lake, Lewis Co., N. Y. I fished by putting down one hundred hooks through holes in the ice about four rods apart. These were baited with good-sized minnows hooked through the back, in such a manner as not to kill them. After the lines had been down the first night, I took from them in the morning twenty-five good-sized salmon trout. Each successive morning thereafter, I took less and less, until on the eighth day the number had diminished to about seven or eight. But the astonishing part of it was, that the bait was gone from every hook just the same as it was on the first morning, when I made the big catch. I knew that the trout were not all caught out, but it was very apparent that I could not catch any more, without removing to a new ground and cutting a new set of holes, which I accordingly did, about a quarter of a mile from my former grounds. There my results were the same as before, and after fishing seven or eight days, I found it would be necessary for me to move again.

One day I ran a line of hooks in such a direction that one of them came over a rocky bar where there was open water. I saw there was an opportunity for an experiment, which I at once decided to try. I fastened the upper end of the line to an overhanging piece of brush, so that nothing could interfere with the bait below without decidedly moving the brush. Then I lay down on the ice with a coat over my head, so that I could look down through the clear water and watch developments. Presently a large, fine trout came along and began manœuvring with the minnow attached to the hook, and operated in the following manner : He kept as close to the minnow as possible, and repeatedly snapped at it very cautiously, re-opening his mouth before he

had fairly closed it, so as to prevent getting anything in his mouth he did not want. When the
lively minnow had swum away far as the line would
permit, the trout made a more forcible snap at it so
as to cut it entirely from the hook. The minnow sank
to the bottom, and the trout went after it and soon
had it stored away. I then discovered why I had to
move so often. I immediately baited the hook with
another minnow and lowered it down; the trout
came for it again and snapped at it as before. I let
it sink to the bottom, where the trout went after it
and swallowed bait, hook, and all, and I never miss-
ed another one; where I saw the trout working at it.

But how came all the trout to adopt the same
plan? I do not believe they could have done so, if
there is not some way by which they can communi-
cate with each other. I have no doubt they would
have had the best of me again, if I had let one get
away, so that he could have held a consultation with
his brethren.

Trout are not the only fish which possess this
reasoning power. We will take the little shad just
hatched, with which many of our rivers have been
restocked, particularly the Hudson and Connecticut,
by the artificial method discovered by myself in the
year 1867. When I deposited them in the river, on
either side, they would start directly for the middle
of the stream. They knew that there were thousands of large minnows which roamed along the
shore to keep out of the way of the larger fish in
the middle of the stream, and that they would eat
up the little shad, which were too small for the
larger fish to notice.

Now if these little fish had not some sort of understanding aside from instinct, I do not think they would have pursued this course to avoid danger.

CHAPTER VIII.

HOW FARMERS CAN RAISE THEIR OWN TROUT.

THERE are many farmers who own trout streams, and would like to have them restocked. Some very feebly attempt to do it by putting in a few thousand young fish. This would restock a small stream if it were done every year successively. But it is folly to suppose that a large stream, which has been fished for years, and thousands taken from it every year, can be restocked quickly by putting in a few hundred, or even a few thousand, young fry.

It is much easier to stock a stream than to raise fish in ponds, because the young fish will take care of themselves much better than any one can take care of them, and if they are protected from danger until they are about forty-five days old—which is about the time the fish culturist takes charge of them—and until they are ready to feed, they are then tolerably able to look out for themselves. In stocking a stream with trout, the young fish should be taken to its head-waters, or put into the springs and little rivulets which empty into it. As they grow larger, they will gradually settle down stream, and run up again to the head-waters in the fall and winter to spawn.

When putting fish into a stream, do not put them suddenly into water much warmer than that of the vessel in which they have been transported. They will not be so likely to be injured by putting them in water a few degrees colder ; but try to avoid all sudden changes, and gradually raise or lower the temperature of the water in which you bring them, until it is even with that of the stream in which they are to be placed. Perhaps in no branch of fish cul-ture are the results more immediate, or more apparent, than in restocking streams. Very many inland streams that were once inhabited by trout, are now wholly depleted, not only of that fish, but of all others. They are beautiful, sparkling little streams, but so far as good food-producing element goes, they are valueless. In a large majority of cases, they will make a wonderful return for the restocking.

In the year 1875, the State of New York directed its Fish Commissioners to purchase a trout-breeding establishment, and to raise and distribute brook trout. Since then, from one to two millions have been hatched and distributed each year, and the results have been most gratifying. Those that were taken first, after the restocking, were small, of course ; those that were left, had the more food, and by the next year, yielded nearly as much weight, although fewer would be taken ; and the following year the fish were still larger, furnishing a splendid return for the expense of restocking.

This addition to the yield of any stream is so

apparent as to convince the most skeptical. It is indisputable; and those who have once visited a trout stream the year after it has been stocked, and have seen the young fish—then from three to five inches in length—darting out from under the weeds and roots, will need no further proof as to the practicability of trout culture. In such cases one may almost say that the number taken from a stream will depend simply upon the number put in, provided the stream is well stocked with food for them, while the cost of hatching and transporting is small, indeed, when compared with the pleasure that is derived.

No brook, that has once contained trout, need be without them, if the waters remain pure and cold. I believe there are no waters more satisfactory to stock than brook-trout streams, because they are always before you. When waters are stocked with shad or salmon, these fish migrate to the ocean, and only return once a year for the purpose of spawning. Salmon-trout and white-fish stay most of the time in the deep waters of our lakes ; but brook-trout remain where they are placed, grow, and are caught, and contribute directly to the support and amusement of the people.

Streams that have been wholly worthless in producing food can be replenished, and be made a very valuable addition to the farm.

CHAPTER IX.

FARMER BOYS AND THE TROUT.

I WANT to tell my young readers something of the habits of brook trout, and how they can aid in their protection and increase their numbers in the streams that flow through their farms. Brook or speckled trout cast their spawn in their natural or wild state, principally from October 15th to December 1st; while in confinement they continue until March 15th.

At this time they frequent the shallow waters at or in the vicinity of the head waters of the streams, where there is a plenty of gravelly bottom on which to deposit their spawn. The males at this time are gaily decked out with their brilliantly spotted coats and beautifully colored crimson fins. The females may be readily distinguished by their more matronly appearance and sombre hues. After they have mated, the female begins to prepare her nest.

Now the point I wish to make, and impress upon the minds of my young readers, is this : While rambling about the farm in the fall, and along the banks of the stream, the trout are frequently discovered in the shallow water, and it is many times an easy task to capture them, and not infrequently they are thrown upon the shore with the hands. This in itself is a great wrong, and as a matter of principle should not be done, any more than you would take the sitting hen from her nest and wring her neck. In each case the act of bringing forth their young is stopped.

By the laws of the State of New York it is illegal to take, kill, catch, or have in possession after the same has been killed, any brook, or speckled trout, from the first day of September to the first day of April in each year, under a penalty of $10 for an attempt, and $25 for each fish so caught, killed, exposed for sale, or had in possession; and a penalty of $50 for disturbing or molesting fish upon their spawning beds, or taking spawn or milt therefrom, with $25 additional for each fish taken thereon.

Although it is unlawful to take trout during the above time, and we all should have due respect for the law, it is not a very difficult matter to destroy a great many trout out of season without being detected, and I hope I may succeed in interesting my young friends to look upon this question as a matter of honor with them, and as something which is for their interest to look after and protect. Certainly there is no other class who can do more good in this direction if they exert their influence in the right way, and none who can do more harm if they are so disposed.

When you have " a day off " to go trout fishing at the proper season, or invite your friends from the city to join you in a day's recreation, your desire is to take some fish, and if the trout are not allowed to breed (unless kept up by artificial planting), the stock will just as surely run out as would your fowls, if they were not given an opportunity for breeding. In addition to protecting trout through their spawning season, a great deal of good work may also be done in cutting brush and scattering it along the edges of the stream. This will form hiding places and protection for the young when they hatch out in the spring. It is not a good plan to cut the trees and bushes away from the shores, as they form shade for the fish and the roots hold the water back, and prevent the streams from drying up.

A great many trout streams have been ruined by cutting away the trees from the head waters, and where they flow through the meadows. By so doing the streams are exposed to the entire heat of the sun during the summer months, which renders the water too warm for the trout and they soon disappear. From sixty-eight to seventy degrees F. is about the limit of warmth of water in which trout can survive, and unless they can have immediate access to the springs feeding the main streams, they will die.

I have no doubt that many of our young readers have heard their fathers tell of the brooks in which they used to fish when they were boys, and of the numbers of the speckled beauties they had drawn from the waters ; but the brooks have now, for the above reasons, become unsuitable for trout, and the haunts which knew them once know them no more ; and so I wish the farmer boys of to-day to profit by the mistakes of their fathers, and protect the trout streams that still remain, before it is too late. Another point to which I wish to call your attention is, to throw back the " fingerling " trout.

Do not save any that are under six inches in length. In another year these will more than

double their weight, and be fish worth taking. Do
not act on the principle that if you do not take
them, some one else will ; but do your share man-
fully, and your good example will, without doubt,
have its effect on others.

CHAPTER X.

THE DISEASES OF FISH.

I AM very often asked the question, Are fish subject to sickness and disease the same as other orders
of creation? My experience with them indicates
that they are. Sickness is not only liable to take
place among individuals, but an epidemic sometimes
breaks out among certain kinds which destroys them
in large numbers, and nothing can be done to check
the scourge, until it has run its course, as is usually the case with cholera, yellow fever and other con-
tagious diseases, when they attack portions of the
human race.

It is quite a singular fact that, when an epidemic
breaks out in any waters, only one kind of fish is
affected at the same time, which shows that the
disease cannot be caused by any impurity of the
waters or any cause of a like nature. If it were,
all the different kinds of fish in that body of water
would be affected in a similar manner.

As is the case with the human race, certain fish
escape the contagion, and it is a pretty good rule

that where they can be taken by angling with hook and line, such fish are safe to eat.

When fish are affected by disease, they almost invariably die; not one in a hundred recovers; and there is at present no known remedy which can be said to be efficacious.

The only effectual remedy which I have known, is a common salt and water bath. I have used it with good results in a few instances with trout. The brine should be made strong enough to float a potato. The sick fish is then placed in it and allowed to remain until it turns over, which will usually occur in a few minutes. It should then be taken out immediately and placed in fresh water. The fish should be immersed in this bath about twice a day, and the operation be repeated about half a dozen times. If this does not cure the fish, you may give it up as a hopeless case.

The disease most common with trout—and I have seen it with other fish as well—makes its appearance in the form of a white fungus growth. It may appear on any part of the body in whitish patches, but spreads rapidly, and soon reaches the head and gills. When it reaches the gills, or breathing apparatus of the fish, the fungus apparently fastens them together, and death is the result. The theory concerning this disease is, that the fungus is a parasitic growth, and the object of the salt and water bath is to kill the parasite. If this is accomplished, the fish stands a chance of recovering, provided it is taken in time.

Concerning the health of fish kept in confinement, the same rules are applicable to them as to ourselves. They must be plentifully supplied with

good water and good food, or else they will lose
their vigor and activity, and soon become thin and
emaciated and die a lingering death.

Of course, there are certain kinds of fish so con-
stituted that they can endure greater hardship than
others, and it was a wise provision of the Creator, to
provide fish which were adapted to the peculiarities
of the different bodies of water, just as He created
mankind, organized so as to be able to withstand the
climate, temperature and atmospheric changes to
which the different parts of the globe are subject.

It is therefore necessary, in the cultivation of fish,
to provide for them the elements their natures require, in order that they may be healthful. As fish
are difficult to cure, the great secret is to properly
care for them, so they may keep free from disease;
in other words, the cure consists in the prevention.
In their wild state, fish undoubtedly die from the
same relative causes as the human race. They are
infested by a variety of parasites, etc. Tape-worms
are not infrequently found in their intestines; on one
occasion I took out of a minnow, not more than three
inches ·long, five tape-worms, measuring, when
stretched full length, from two to two and a half
inches. They occupied at least two-thirds of the
abdominal cavity. I took this fish on a small hook,
and it did not seem to be inconvenienced by the
extra load it was carrying. I have also found worms
imbedded in the solid flesh along the back of the
fish.

Another disease which I have observed in trout is
the growth of tubercles in the gills. When these had
attained a size so as to separate the gills and inter-

fere with their normal action, death was the result. These tubercles seemed to be filled with a watery matter, and thus it appears that the inhabitants of the watery kingdom are, like ourselves, subject to aches and pains and many diseases, and, like ourselves, perish because of them.

CHAPTER XI.

MALFORMATION OF FISH FRY.

FEW persons are aware that the young of fish, when first ushered into this world, are as liable to unshapeliness as are all other orders of creation. Indeed, some of them are even more peculiarly formed in some respects than any other living creature. But the good Lord has ordained, as the fate of all deformed fish fry, that they shall cease to live after a certain number of days, rarely ever exceeding thirty, and in the majority of cases not as many.

The causes through which these singular freaks are brought into existence are undoubtedly due to the violation of some of the unchangeable laws of nature. I have never taken the trouble to ascertain accurately just what proportion of the young fish which have passed under my observation are thus deformed, but the percentage is very small, and, at a rough estimate, I should say about one in five thousand. With the varieties of fish I have hatched artifically, those among which most of the deformities occur are the brook and salmon trout ; rather more of the former than of the latter. I can account for this on no other ground than from the fact that as a rule the brook-trout inhabit small bodies of water, thereby rendering the possibilities of inter-breeding greater than with other fish. In any event, the percentage is so small that it in no sense interferes with the results of artificial propagation. The two kinds of malformations most frequent among the young fry, are those with two heads and one body or trunk, and those known as Siamese Twins, from the fact of their being connected similarly to that celebrated monstrosity. Rare cases occur, where the fish have three heads on one body. Among the millions of young fry that have passed under my observation, I have seen but two specimens of this kind.

The fry are also subject to all sorts of curvatures of the back-bones. The curves are found at nearly all degrees, from a slight bend to a complete circle— the head and tail meeting. Some that are affected in this way are able to swim, but they go round and round in a continuous circle. Others are so knotted as to be unable to make any progress whatever. The cause of death in these instances is the absorption of the yolk sac which is attached to each young fry. While this remains, food is unnecessary, and it will sustain life in the deformed fry for about thirty days, and in a healthy fish for about forty days. When it is gone, the former die of starvation, as they are unable to find food. For the sake of the experiment, I have tried to prolong their lives by careful feeding, and have succeeded in so doing for about sixty days, after which they succumb. One pecu-

liarity is that the malformed fry have a tendency tow-
ard a superabundance of heads rather than of tails.
I have never found a specimen with more than its
share of caudal appendage.

Albinism is not unfrequent. The fish are perfect
albinos in every respect, even to the pink eyes.
These I have raised, and they are really beautiful little creatures, and when placed in a glass jar, every
bone and fiber in their nearly transparent bodies,
fins and tails, can be plainly discerned. The great
trouble in keeping them in ponds is that they show
up so distinctly that they make an excellent target
for king-fishers and fish-hawks, which, in spite of all
our watchfulness, are almost sure to capture them
sooner or later. One of the albinos I kept until it
was three years old, when from some unknown cause
it died. It was a female fish, from which I took
three hundred spawn, a good percentage of which
hatched, but the young fry showed no peculiarities
different from other trout.

CHAPTER XII.

A LESSON IN FISH CULTURE.

I AM almost daily in receipt of inquiries : "How
may I best obtain practical information on the cultivation of fish ?" First of all, I recommend reading,
so far as possible, good works on the subject. By so
doing, you will be saved many vexations and trials,

and avoid the failures and mistakes made by those who were obliged to learn by hard study and experience. When I first began practical fish culture, I had but very little of this literature to guide me, and consequently it often took me considerable time to work out problems which now appear very simple.

After you have informed yourself about the necessary requirement for success, commence by obtaining a few spawn or fish, and make your first experiments in a small way. Although you may be well versed theoretically, you will find, in attempting to make an actual application of your knowledge, that you will meet with obstacles you did not dream of before ; in other words, you must educate your hands as well as your head to do the work.

Commence in a small way, and conduct your first experiments as cheaply as possible. "But why?" you may say. "I have read up thoroughly on the subject, and the path seems clear enough. Why let a year go by without doing work, that will amount to something?" My friend, could you reasonably expect to read how to make a clock, or any other piece of machinery, and then sit down and make it? There are, undoubtedly, geniuses who are able to do this, but they are the exception, and not the rule. The chances are even, that you will make some fatal mistake the first season, and your experience will be just as valuable, and not nearly so expensive, if you start on a small scale. A great deal can be learned by visiting some establishment which is in successful operation, and the observations made there will be of great value to the beginner.

Many failures occur through the impression that fish culture is so very simple. This is a great mistake, as to conduct it successfully requires constant attention, the same as any other business. The value of experimenting and making practical tests cannot be too highly estimated. There are so many things which to your vision look clear and practical, which an actual trial will prove to be useless. Theoretically they may be true, but practically failures. I have many times caught an idea which seemed to be just the thing, and must prove a success, and found I was wrong, so that my usual plan now is, when I undertake to solve a difficult problem, to have several different experiments under way at the same time, and among them will be some which I had made up my mind would be certain failures, and many times some one of these would be just the thing I wanted.

There are many waters where it is impossible to tell whether certain fish will live without putting some in and giving them a trial. For instance, if one wishes to stock a stream that is impregnated with some kind of mineral—perhaps iron or sulphur—he would have no way of knowing how strongly the waters were impregnated, or just what degree of strength the fish could endure. In this case I would advise placing a few fish in the waters in question as a sure means of ascertaining. Of course, there are certain kinds of fish which, if deposited in waters having the necessary temperature, depth, bottom, etc., will almost to a certainty thrive if placed therein. There are waters possessing such characteristics that we know that certain fish will not live in them ; but when the waters are such that it is a matter of doubt, the correct way is to experiment.

A new beginner cannot expect to learn it all the first year, or the second. The more he studies and experiments, the more he will find there is to learn ; in fact, fish culture does not differ from any other business in this respect. I have been working at practical fish culture for about twenty-four years, and had it on my mind since the year 1837, and I find there is still a great deal to be learned and discovered about fish and how to raise them.

CHAPTER XIII.

WRONG IMPRESSIONS IN FISH CULTURE.

THERE are a great many wrong impressions concerning the cultivation of fish; and, with this idea in view, I will try and explain to my readers some of the false opinions which I find have been formed in the minds of people with whom I have come in contact.

One of the most prevalent errors is, that if a person controls a body of water, a lake, stream or pond, as the case may be, that he can, through the medium of fish culture, raise, or keep in confinement any kind of fish his fancy dictates. Now if the tillers of the soil will think how unreasonable it would be for any one to suppose for an instant, that he could produce any kind of grain or fruit on any kind of soil he chose, he will readily comprehend his mistake in regard to fish. The Creator, in His wise distribution of things on the earth's surface, placed them with an eye to their adaptability to the quarters to which they were assigned. He did not place whales in the inland lakes, or sturgeons in the small spring streams, but He placed them in the bodies of water where there was room and food in abundance for them, and which were suited to their peculiarities. He placed in the small spring streams the brook or speckled trout, which do not grow to a great size, and, as a consequence, the food intended for them can be produced in sufficient quantities to sustain them. He placed the sturgeon in our large inland lakes and rivers, and the enormous leviathan in the ocean. I have purposely taken the extremes in my illustration, so as to better demonstrate my meaning ; but there are many fishes in the intermediate class which, as a rule, grow and increase in proportion to the abundance of food and extent of the waters they inhabit, to the limit in size to which Nature. has designed they should attain.

And so in fish culture there is nothing visionary, or theoretical, or in conflict with Nature's laws. It is only by working with Nature and assisting her that we can hope to succeed ; the very moment we deviate from this path, failure is sure to follow. If you transfer the bass from the river or bay to the brook, and the trout from the brook to the bay, they will not thrive, because the elements are not there which their nature requires.   It is only by aiding Nature in her unchangeable course that success is attained.

Another point which has frequently come to my notice is, that in the artificial manipulation of fish, the erroneous impression has been gained by many intelligent people, that young fry can be produced from the eggs of a fish in which life had departed. It is my opinion, based upon actual experiment, that the eggs cannot be vitalized, after the heart has ceased to beat.   To test this matter correctly, it is necessary to wait some time—an hour at least—after the fish has ceased to exhibit any outward signs of life; as I have ascertained by examining young fry under the microscope, that the blood will flow and the heart beat for twenty minutes to a half hour after the fish is to all outward appearances dead. In order to obtain the best results from artificial impregnation, both parent fish must be alive and in a healthy condition, and the eggs fully matured naturally.   If the eggs are forced from the fish prematurely, the operation will result in failure and the fish thus operated upon will almost always die.

Another false idea, which is by no means uncommon, is that fish can live and thrive without food. This is a mistake ; fish require food the same as any other living creature, and in abundance, according to their size.   This wrong impression has been gained through keeping gold fish in aquariums in which they have been known to live for months, and in some cases years, without putting in food ; but the means through which they live is by sucking the greenish matter from the sides of the aquarium and

stones. This matter contains microscopic plants
and animals, on which they subsist. In cleaning an
aquarium in which gold fish are kept, never wash the
stones, but take·them out carefully, and replace
them without disturbing the slimy substance on
them.

CHAPTER XIV.

ARTIFICIAL HATCHING OF FISH.

IN the artificial hatching of fish eggs, there are
three principal conditions necessary, without which
success can rarely be attained. These are cleanliness, careful handling of the eggs and plenty of
circulation. The importance of providing these can
hardly be over-estimated.

CLEANLINESS.—One of the main reasons why
artificial propagation is superior to the natural
method is in this particular. The eggs must be
kept free from sediment or dirt in any form whatever, or else they can never reach the hatching
point. We will take the clear, flowing brook as we
observe it casually: it has the appearance of being
free from all foreign substance, but, by examining it
closely, we discover that in the bed of the brook a
great deal of matter is constantly moving downward. This has the tendency to cover up all eggs
which have been cast, and, when this occurs, the
egg will never come to maturity. In hatching eggs
artificially, this is guarded against by filtering the
water through flannel screens, and also by having a

large tank into which the water flows before entering the hatchery. This gives the impurities a
chance to settle at the bottom, and the water will
become purer ; and when it afterward flows through
the flannel screens, it is purified to a still greater extent. But, even with these precautions, a great deal
of sediment will force itself through into the hatching apparatus, and the eggs have to be looked over
and feathered nearly every day in order to keep
them bright and clean. The hatching apparatus itself needs frequent washing to keep it free from the
matter which accumulates on it. Without scrupu-
lous cleanliness, artificial propagation would not, in
this respect, be superior to the natural.

CAREFUL HANDLING.—This, in my opinion, is a
most important consideration, and one that cannot
be over-estimated. Some persons claim that there
are stages in the development of the eggs when
they can be handled very roughly, and will stand a
great deal of abuse without injury. This is con-
trary to my experience. From the time the egg is
first taken, until it is hatched, the utmost caution
should be taken to prevent any ill-usage. While
there is undoubtedly a certain period when the eggs
are less liable to be killed by exposure to some
amount of hardship than at other times, still, I find
that the most careful treatment given them is none
too good ; and the more gentle we are with them
the larger percentage of strong and vigorous fish
breaks through the shell of the egg. Even in
"feathering" them over with the bearded side of a
feather in search for dead eggs, it would be better if
the eggs were not touched, but simply moved by

the agitation of the water. It is also important that the eggs should always be entirely under water while examining them. "Handle with care" is an injunction the common sense and value of which will demonstrate itself to anyone, as his experience in fish culture extends.

FREE CIRCULATION.—The object to be kept in view, in the construction of apparatus for hatching fish eggs is, to have it so arranged that the eggs or spawn will receive the constant action of flowing water without being washed away. By "plenty of circulation," is meant sufficient to keep the eggs slightly in motion, but not enough to move them violently. The eggs of some fishes are much lighter than those of others. For instance, those of the trout and salmon are much heavier, and more bulky, than those of the shad or white-fish. Consequently, different apparatus has to be used in the hatching of different kinds of fishes. A successful fish-hatching apparatus should be so constructed that the water will circulate freely around each individual egg, and this current must not be allowed to cease from the time the eggs are first put in until the fishes are hatched. Absence of circulation results in sure death to the eggs, and this is one of the reasons why so few eggs, cast naturally, produce a fish. The egg must be fortunate, indeed, to become located in as favorable a position as can be given to it under artificial propagation.

Taking into consideration the number of eggs cast by all kinds of fish, I do not believe the average of those hatched is more than one in a thousand, and this is a liberal estimate.

CHAPTER XV.

THE PROTECTION OF FISH.

I AM in receipt of a letter from a correspondent, concerning the protection of fish. He says: "I am much interested in your researches. I never caught a fish in my life, but can appreciate the importance of protecting our fish from the unthinking or selfish who despoil our rivers and streams." The matter of protecting our fish is a subject which should interest every good citizen, whether he be a fisherman or not; it is a question which concerns the food supply of the country, a matter of vital importance to every man, woman and child.

Now I propose to show how fish are destroyed by the unthinking, or the class of men who do not care whether there are any fish left in the waters or not, so long as they manage to transfer a few paltry dollars to their pockets, which, as a rule, do them little or no good.

The fishermen who do the most damage are those who take the fish during their spawning seasons. It is at this time that the fish come into shallow water to complete their work of procreation, and are then easily captured. All fish have certain localities to which they resort at the season of the year when their eggs are matured and ready to cast. Different varieties seek different localities; as, for instance, the speckled or brook trout cast their spawn on the gravel; the lake or salmon trout on rocky reefs; the pickerel and perch among the weeds; the bull-head in holes excavated by them in the mud, etc. These localities are well known to poachers, and where the fish congregate in these places in large schools, they draw nets around them and frequently capture the whole lot at a single haul. Where the bottom is such that it is impracticable to draw a seine by reason of its being covered with boulders or rocky reefs, the "gill net" is used.

This net is made of very fine thread, and the meshes of the net are made in proportion to the size of the fish intended to be captured, and as the name of the net implies, the fish, while swimming through the water, thrust their heads into the meshes of the net, which catch them under their gills and hold them securely. If, by any chance, the fish should succeed in freeing itself from the net, it does not stand one chance in a hundred of recovering; the reason of which is that the gills are, comparatively speaking, the fish's lungs. When the fish feels himself caught, he instinctively struggles violently to escape, thereby lacerating his breathing apparatus to a great extent. We all know the usual result of injury to our own lungs, and it will, therefore, be easy to comprehend the effect upon fish.

Another method by which our inland waters are deprived of hundreds of thousands of young fish annually, is through the means of the murderous spear and jack-light. The depredators approach at night the spawning beds of the salmon trout, bass or other fish; the strong light of the jack, as it is called, thrown upon the water, enables the spearman to see down in the clear water for several feet;

the darkness of the night serves in the same way as a cloak thrown over the head in the day-time, in looking below the ice, through which means objects can be seen a considerable distance down. The fish have apparently little fear of the light, and the boat is easily paddled up to within a few feet of them, when the deadly spear is used. Not only are many captured in this way, but many are injured which are not brought to the boat, so that they die by being pierced by the tines of the spear, and death is the result in a few hours or days, according to the injury.

There are also several other ways by which fish are destroyed while on their spawning beds, as by shooting, snaring, etc., but I think I have explained the matter sufficiently, and trust it will make an impression on the minds of my readers, so that they will exert their influence to protect the fish from illegal modes of capture at all times, and their wholesale destruction, particularly when they are on their spawning beds.

CHAPTER XVI.

CONSTRUCTION OF TROUT PONDS.

THE most necessary requirement for the construction of a trout pond is a plentiful supply of pure spring water. The spring—or springs, if there are several—should have a fall of two or three feet, and if more than one pond is to be made, a fall of from five to ten feet would be an advantage. If the water supply is abundant, there is less necessity for fall. The water from a spring near its source remains at nearly the same temperature during the whole year, and is therefore the best for trout raising. Brook water which does not rise higher than sixty-eight degrees Fahrenheit during the hottest summer months, may be used to supply ponds for adult trout. If the water remains cool enough only during ten months or even more in the year, and then during a dry time gets warmer, it causes the death of all the fish.

It is not, as a rule, a good plan, by damming up a stream, to make ponds that vary in volume. There should be enough level land by the side of such a stream to make ponds to be supplied by the stream, and it is best to have a stream much greater in volume than is necessary for the ponds. This will always furnish a good supply of water, and there will be no trouble with the surplus in case of a freshet.

It is desirable to have the pond as near the dwelling house as possible. You will then be able to give the fish more care and attention than if the pond was at greater distance. Another reason, and quite an important one, too, for having the pond near the house, is, that it may then be guarded against poachers. There are many men who would have no particular conscientious scruples against quietly stealing to your pond at night and drawing a net through it, after you have it nicely stocked. There have been many instances of this kind, and too much caution cannot be exercised in this respect. A good watch dog in the vicinity of the pond will prove a valuable protector.

Trout ponds should be made too small rather than too large; the fish will be found to thrive much better in small than in large ponds. The water supply may be cool enough on entering the pond to sustain the trout during the entire year, but by spreading it over a large space, it presents too much surface to the sun and consequently becomes very warm. Although in such cases the trout will, through the instinct of self-preservation, gather in the vicinity of the inlet and springs, if there are any in the ponds, and save themselves, as far as possible, the result will be the loss of many. When it becomes desirable to construct a pond in a place where there are springs, or to dam up the water and make a pond in a springy place, it is a good plan to cover the springs with several loads of gravel, for the fish to spawn on. The borders of such a pond should be made very shallow, so that the little fish may run up in the shallow water and escape the large fish, or have the pond so arranged that after the fish have spawned, the large ones may be removed. By so doing, the eggs will hatch out and the young fish will grow without danger. When the next season of spawning comes, the little fish may be removed into another pond and the old ones let in to spawn again. Such a pond is specially adapted for persons who cannot devote a great deal of time to it, and who desire to manage it with as little care as possible. In this way a good many fish can be raised without much trouble. The gravel must be sifted and all the fine parts rejected;

none smaller than a hickory nut should be used, and from that to a good-sized hen's egg.

Not infrequently the bottom of such a pond is porous, and absorbs the water nearly as fast as it runs in, so that there is but little if any overflow at the proper outlet. If you are short of water and wish to use all you can possibly get for another pond, or for other purposes, it is best to cement the bottom. But if you have no further use for the water, it makes no difference how it goes off, provided there are no holes in the bottom large enough to let the fish escape, and the water keeps up to its level. In case the water should prove too warm for trout, such a pond would answer for bass, perch, gold fish, or carp.

CHAPTER XVII.

PONDS FOR ARTIFICIAL PROPAGATION OF TROUT.

There are scarcely two locations that present exactly the same conditions for the construction of trout ponds, and where the same plans could be carried out with equal success. Perhaps the best system for economizing water and space, and which at the same time is the most convenient for changing the fish from one pond to another, is to build a series of four or six ponds.

Make them entirely of wood. The plan I have adopted is to build them two abreast, and the others following in order. Each should be about twenty

feet long, by twelve feet wide, and five feet deep.
Unmatched hemlock lumber, an inch or an inch and
one-half in thickness, is suitable for the purpose.
The ground is measured and staked off to the desired dimensions. The excavation is made as if for
one pond, and stakes are driven at regular intervals,
a few feet apart, around the entire excavation. If
the bottom is made of lumber—which is necessary
if the ground is porous—that should be laid first ;
scantling should run across the bottom and be attached to the stakes around the sides of the pond,
upon which to lay the bottom. If the bottom is
made of lumber, the pond can be kept cleaner and
the water is always clear. After the bottom is laid,
the sides should be enclosed with planks running
lengthwise, and not straight up and down, for the
reason that the wood between " wind and water " is
always the first to decay. By placing the planks
lengthwise, new ones can be substituted with but
little expense ; whereas if the boards are in perpen-
dicular position, it would necessitate an entire
change of lumber.

A double partition extends through the centre of
the excavation ; the space between the sides should
be about two feet in width and filled in with earth.
This strengthens the sides of the ponds, and also
affords a walk between them. The two sides are
then partitioned off into compartments of equal
sizes. The ponds on each side of the central divi-
sion should have openings of about three feet in
width between them, into which screens should be
introduced, so as to keep the fish separate and yet
allow the water to flow through. The screens

should be so arranged that they can be readily removed, when it becomes desirable to give the fish
the range of two or more ponds.

At the head of each side of the ponds the spawning races should be located, and through these the
water that feeds the ponds should flow. The race-
ways should be about thirty feet in length and
four feet wide ; the depth of the water flowing
through them should be about six inches. The
sides of the raceway should be made of one and a
half inch plank and about eighteen inches in depth.
This raceway must be filled with coarse gravel, of
the size of a hickory nut to a hen's egg. The bottom of the pond must slope gently up to the raceway. The head of the race should be carefully
screened, and the screens kept clean, so as to prevent the fish from escaping. It is desirable to
bring the water into the race through a long box,
as the water will very soon work around or under a
short box, and allow the fish to escape. If the
water enters with a fall, it may be allowed to pour
over an apron constructed of slats, one-half or one-
quarter of an inch apart, and set edgewise. This
will let the water through and keep the fish from
running up. Trout will run up stream very freely
and work their way through a very small passage,
but are not so likely to run down stream.

The outlet of the pond should also be carefully
screened. The screens may be made of common
wire, and painted with tar mixed with one-third
turpentine or to the consistency of paint. They
may also be made of copper or galvanized wire
sieving. Wire screens for keeping the small fry

should be fourteen threads to the inch, and for one-year olds five or six threads to the inch. The frames of the screens should be fitted in grooves and made to fit as close as possible and still admit of their being easily removed. A good screen for two and three year olds and for larger fish, can be made of strips of lath nailed to a strong frame, with quarter-inch openings between them. The slats should be four inches wide, so that if a leaf strikes against them it will catch or pass through without obstructing the flow of water, or lie flat against a single slat. If the slats are narrow, the leaves will lop around them and clog up the screen.

CHAPTER XVIII.

CARP ON THE FARM.

IN reply to several inquiries about carp culture, the following condensed directions are given, as undoubtedly many are interested in this subject.

To construct a pond, first stake off your land the desired dimensions ; then take a plow and scraper, and with them make the necessary excavation. The pond should be about five or six feet deep in the centre, gradually sloping up to the edges. The object in having the pond deep in the centre is to provide the fish with a place to settle into during the winter, without danger of the water freezing solid and thereby killing them, as would be the

case in cold climates if the water was all shallow.
The reason for having the bottom sloping is, that
thereby the fish may have access to plenty of warm,
shoal water, and also, that in case the old fish
are not taken out after spawning, the young will
have the protection of the shallow water along the
edges, into which the larger fish cannot swim if
they should feel inclined to make a meal on some
of their younger relatives.

The outlet should be about three feet wide, and
so constructed that it can be well screened to prevent the fish from escaping, and so as to admit of
the water being drawn off when it is desired to re-
move the fish or to cleanse the pond. The screens
may be made of wire netting, and painted with
gas-tar mixed with one-third turpentine, or to the
consistency of paint, and applied with an ordinary
paint brush. The wire netting should be tacked to
strong wooden frames, made to fit the space to be
screened. To screen a carp pond effectually, three
screens of different sized meshes should be used.
These should slide in a grooved framework, so
that they can be taken out easily and cleaned.
The coarser screen should be placed first, or nearest
to the pond, so as to catch the principal part of
the drifting matter, and prevent the clogging of
the lower and finer screens. About eighteen inches
back of the screens the outlet boards should be
placed, fitted to slide in a groove. They should be
about six inches wide each, and made to fit closely,
as it is by these that the overflow is regulated.

It is advisable to have the top boards narrower
than the lower ones, so that the water may be

raised or lowered to any level desired. If galvanized wire—which is the best, although more expensive—is used for screens, it need not be painted with gas-tar. For a pond containing large carp only, the outlet screen may be made of slats about three inches wide, with half-inch openings between the slats. If a leaf strikes against slats of this width, it will pass between them without obstructing the flow of water, as it cannot lap around them, as it would do if the slats were smaller. In all cases the screens should extend nearly to the bottom of the pond, so as to present as great a surface as possible.

Carp can be raised in well water, but water from a brook is preferable. They will succeed in the Northern States, if the ponds are deep enough not to freeze to the bottom in winter. Carp do not require feeding in winter, as they burrow into the mud or hibernate, until the ice disappears in the spring.

There appears to be a difference of opinion among the authorities as to which is the best kind of carp. The scale carp are said to be the most prolific, and the leather carp grow the fastest. For my part I prefer the latter ; it is the handsomer and finer fish of the two. As to their qualities as table fish, so far as my experience goes, I have not been able to discover any difference between them.

CHAPTER XIX.

VALUE OF COMMON FISH.

I WISH to say a few words concerning the great value and usefulness of what are usually termed the "common varieties" of fish. These include the yellow perch, rock bass, bull-head, sucker, pickerel, and the like. These fish, though they do not command the attention of writers and fish-culturists, as trout, salmon, black bass, white fish, and shad do, still hold a very important place in the fish-supply of the country, and furnish pleasure and food for many thousands of people.

The class of fish above referred to do not require the care and attention to make them plentiful, that is necessary with the finer or game varieties. Artificial propagation is not required, and about the only thing really needed to keep a plentiful supply in the waters to which they are adapted, is to protect them while they are in their spawning-beds, and fish for them only by angling by hand, with hook and line. In this way you get the greatest amount of actual enjoyment in the capture of the fish; and who is there that does not relish a mess of fish caught by himself, better than those purchased, or procured in any other way?

Another point concerning these common fish is that, as a rule, they are easily caught, and it requires no especially fine tackle to take them, though the most successful fishermen are careful in the arrangements of their hooks and lines, and also keep their hook properly sharpened, and well baited. A common cane pole, such as can be purchased for a small sum, will be found equally as serviceable as a high-priced, split bamboo, jointed rod. These fish also inhabit large rivers, lakes and bays, which are accessible to the millions. They are also found in the canals, to which thousands resort in summer for the capture of a mess of fish. In such waters as these, the finer grades of fish cannot live and thrive. Therefore the ordinary bull-head, with his great powers of endurance, is a welcome and valuable inhabitant of this class of waters. The yellow perch, with its white, flaky flesh, when properly cooked, is the equal of any common fish in the country. I have made many a good meal on the usually underrated sucker and mullet.

A great many harsh things are said against the pickerel, but it is a good fish, and a worthy inhabitant of the kind of water in which it is found. It is not a suitable companion for the trout, nor is there a sufficiency of food for it in trout waters, but there is plenty in our large lakes, rivers and bays, and many a day's sport have I had pickerel fishing. As a table-fish, the pickerel is not, in my opinion, equal to the yellow perch or bull-head, but when properly prepared it is very palatable. While pickerel do not possess the game qualities of the muscalonge, still in some waters I have found them to have considerable "fight," and one of eight or ten pounds weight affords both sport and an exercise of skill to land.

Who has not seen a row of bare-footed urchins

sitting on a bridge or the bank of a stream, angling
for suckers ? And what a happy expression they
bear on their faces, when they trudge home with a
string long enough to drag on the ground ! Many a
great man, and angler as well, has taken his first les
sons in fishing from catching the slow-going fish that
gains his subsistence by sucking the nutriment from
the stones on the bottom of the stream.

The value of our common fresh-water varieties is
very great. They come in where they are most
needed, and with our extensive watered area, no one
need be denied the privilege of fishing, or cultivating
a love for this harmless and healthful pastime. When
the head of the family decides to take the little ones
out fishing, and they are all gathered in the boat,
each one furnished with a rod, no salmon fisherman,
with his rod bending under the strain of a twenty-
pound salmon, enjoys the fun with a keener delight
than the parents and children, as the perch and rock-
bass come flopping in over the side of the boat.

CHAPTER XX.

ANGLING FOR BLACK BASS.

MANY who delight in angling, have doubtless caught
the black bass. I do not know of any one fish that is so
general a favorite with anglers as the genuine Small-
Mouthed Black Bass. He is so game and full of
pluck that he excites your admiration, and when

you have at last landed him, you feel that you have conquered a foeman worthy of your steel.

There are two kinds of fish known as the Black Bass, but they are quite different in their nature and habits. They are known as the Small-Mouthed Black Bass, and the Large-Mouthed or Oswego Bass. The latter, as the name implies, has the largest mouth, and lives in still water where weeds, flags and pond-lilies are plentiful. He is caught quite readily at still fishing, using minnows for bait, and is also captured by trolling along the edge of the weeds with the spoon and minnow, attached to a gang of hooks. The latter is my favorite way of fishing for them. The big-mouthed black bass is the poorer table-fish of the two kinds, and does not possess the game qualities of the small-mouthed variety, which lives only in pure lake or river water with rocky bottom. They are taken still-fishing with the dobson, also known as the hell-gramite, the craw-fish, or fresh-water crab, and the minnow. These three are undoubtedly the best baits for fishing from an anchored boat.

In my opinion, the finest way to take them, and that which gives the most sport, is by trolling with the following described rig: I use a nine-foot single gut leader, and attached thereto are two flies, tied on a good-sized hook, not smaller than a No. 1 or larger than a 1-0, and a gang of hooks on the end. The leader is made in two parts; the part to which the line is attached is six feet long; then a small swivel—number 8 or 9—is placed between, and then the remainder of the leader.

I have used hundreds of different kinds of flies, and

have kept sifting them out until I have now but four kinds. If I use but two flies on my leader, my upper one is a red body, white wing, and white hackle and a gold tinsel stripe. My second is called the "grizzly king." It has a green body, and a mottled wing of a mallard or red-head. It is called by fly-makers the under wing ; it has a grizzly hackle and red ibis tail. My two other flies are called the "Governor Alvord" and "Seth Green." The wing of the former is made of two colored feathers, cinnamon and drab. The cinnamon is used for the under part of the wing. The body is made of peacock hackle and a red ibis tail. The "Seth Green" is made as follows : The body is green with a large yellow stripe. The hackle red, from the red rooster. The wing is made of feathers out of a bittern or woodcock, or any cinnamon-color wing. I do not cover the body of my flies with hackle ; the hackle is all put on at the head of the fly.

The gang of hooks is made as follows : Use No. 8 "O'Shaughnessy hooks;" solder two sets of three hooks each, back to back, in the shape of a grapnel, and tie them on a single gut, having the first set on the end and the next from one to two inches above, and a short distance above, tie a single lip-hook. The gangs should be made to fit the size of the minnows used ; attach the minnow to the gang by hooking the upper or lip-hook through both lips, which closes the mouth ; insert one of the lower hooks in the side near the tail, and one of the middle set, in the side. The minnow should have a very slight curve when on the gang, which will give it a slow rotary motion when drawn through the water.

Use a rod and multiplying reel, with about one hundred and fifty feet of line on it, but the length of line used in actual fishing is usually from forty to seventy-five feet, depending on the depth of water. In fishing in twelve feet of water, I would use seventy-five feet of line, and put two No. 1 split-shot on my leader. In still-fishing with minnow, and holding the rod in hand, hook the minnow through both lips; fish near the bottom and give it short starts ahead. When still-fishing with a cork, measure the depth of the water and place the cork on your line, so that the hook will be within one or two feet of the bottom, and hook your minnow through the middle of the back, being very careful not to touch the back-bone, and throw your line out as far as you can.

When the bass goes for your bait ne goes with a rush, and when he strikes it, will probably go three or four feet before he stops. Then he will turn the minnow in his mouth and proceed to swallow it, and as it is going down he will start to swim off slowly; then is the time to strike.

If you will follow these directions you will miss but very few bites, but if you strike when the cork first begins to bob, you will lose your fish more than half the time. In hooking on craw-fish, insert your hook through the under side of the tail, near the body, and have the hook come out on the back. Lengthen out your line so that it touches bottom, and it is a good plan to cripple the crab by breaking off one or his claws, or raise him a little off the bottom occasionally. Otherwise he is liable to crawl under stones and hide.

CHAPTER XXI.

THE STURGEON.

THIS fish is fast becoming extinct, and I dare say that the time will come when mounted specimens will be carried through the country along with other curiosities which usually accompany a menagerie. The sturgeon is the largest species of fish that inhabits the fresh water lakes of this country. It grows to a length of six feet, and in some instances more, and frequently weighs over a hundred pounds. It is also found in the large rivers flowing into the ocean, and there attains a greater size than the fresh-water variety. I have heard of specimens weighing as heavy as four hundred pounds.

During summer it is a great sight to see sturgeons leaping from the water. They come straight up, and look, at a distance, like great logs shooting up full length above the surface of the water. This they do, without doubt, for their amusement, as, by the peculiar construction of their mouths, they cannot obtain their food from the surface, as do many kinds of fish, and I can, therefore, assign no other cause for this strange action. Their mouth is located on the under side of the head, and is toothless. They obtain their food by means of suction ; that is, they suck their food from off the bottom, and do not grasp it, as do other fish except those belonging to the sucker or carp families. The food of the sturgeon consists of shell-fish, crabs, shrimp, and insects, which by means of his long snout he is able to unearth.

These immense fishes are caught principally in the large pound nets, also in seines, and sometimes in gill nets set for smaller fish. In the latter, in attempting to pass, they get tangled and roll themselves up so that they cannot escape, and frequently break the nets badly. They are also caught by set lines. As food, when properly prepared, they are very good, and highly prized by many. They were at one time so plentiful in the Hudson River, that the flesh was familiarly known as "Albany beef," because of the resemblance of the flesh to beef rather than fish, and by reason of their being marketed and shipped from the capital of New York State in large quantities. Great numbers of them are smoked after they have been pickled in brine, and, prepared in this way, they are an excellent relish. The sturgeon has large quantities of eggs, and, when made into the Russian dish called "caviare," is considered a great delicacy. From the waste parts of the fish and the entrails, quite a large quantity of oil is extracted, and from their bladders isinglass is manufactured.

One of the great enemies of the sturgeon, aside from man, is the lamprey eel, which attaches itself to the body of the fish and sucks its blood. After relinquishing its hold, it leaves a raw sore, which upon healing leaves a permanent good-sized scar on the body. The fish cast their spawn principally during the month of June. We have propagated them artificially in the Hudson River, but not to the extent desired, on account of the scarcity of the fish and the consequent great difficulty in getting a pair together at the same time which were in a perfectly ripe or mature condition for casting and fertilizing the ova. As I have said above, the sturgeon yields large quantities of eggs, it not being an uncommon thing to obtain from a single specimen as high as from fifty to sixty pounds of solid eggs. The eggs are of a dark brown color, and seven of them placed side by side will measure an inch. They will hatch in from three to four days, in water ranging in temperature from sixty-seven to seventy-four degrees.

The eggs when taken from the fish are very glutinous, and adhere to each other, and to everything they touch. The only way they can be kept separate is, by constantly stirring them for from thirty minutes to two hours, after which the gummy substance appears to dissolve. When the young break through the shell, they are very helpless little creatures. One peculiarity is noticeable on the part of the fish in the egg, that it is able to move only the middle part of the body, while with other fish the tail is the principal part most moved. The yolk sac, which is attached to the body is unusually small for young fry, and is absorbed in about six days, after which the fish seeks its own livelihood.

There is no doubt that sturgeons can be largely increased in the great lakes by artificial propagation, provided they are kept in pens until they are in proper condition to operate with. The great drawback to penning them in tide waters, is that the small eels destroy the eggs, by entering the fish through the vent.

CHAPTER XXII.

THE TRANSPORTATION OF FISH.

DOUBTLESS most people are familiar with the milk-can, but probably few know the important part it plays in fish culture. The cans are used for the transportation of fish, and in all my experience I have never found anything better or more convenient to handle. In shape the cans are like those used by milkmen in delivering milk, and not like the regular dairy can with straight sides. The trouble with these is that the water slops about so as to endanger the lives of young fry, in case they should swim to the top of the water. With mature or full-grown fish they will answer the purpose very well.

Our cans will hold about thirteen gallons, but about eleven gallons of water is all that is placed in the cans when fish are being transported, the remainder of the room being left for aeration. The bottoms of the cans are made perfectly flat on the inside, as experience has shown us that in transporting young fry, if the bottoms are oval or crowning, the fry are very liable to settle about the edges on top of each other, and unless they are constantly watched and stirred, the under ones will smother. With the flat bottom this danger is avoided in a great measure. Young fry should not be shipped until the yolk sac is sufficiently absorbed, so that they can swim about in the can.

Besides the can above described, an ordinary water pail and large tin dipper are necessary ; also a piece of rubber tubing with about a five-eighths inch opening, to be used as a siphon in drawing off the water. When it is necessary to change the water the rubber hose is inserted in a tin tube about three inches in diameter, and in length within six or eight inches of the length of the can, inside. The tube is perforated with fine pin holes for about six inches up from the bottom of the tube. This is to admit the water. The upper part of the tube is funnel-shaped, with the opening large enough to admit the siphon. A hook is soldered on the top of the tube, which is caught over the rim of the can, when it is inserted for use. I presume most readers have had occasion to use a siphon, the operation of which is very simple. When the rubber hose is placed in the tube as far as it will go, place the mouth over the end hanging outside the can, and suck the water into the hose until it is nearly full, then suddenly drop it down, so that the end, outside is lower than the inside end of the hose. The water will run until the desired quantity is removed, when the tube may be taken out and new water put in.

The object in not having the tube the full length of the can, is to prevent all the water from being accidentally drawn off, and thus leave the fish stranded. It is not well to give the fish a full change of water, which is liable to prove very injurious, and has been the means of killing a good many fish while being transported. The idea is to keep the temperature of the water as nearly even as possible, and if it is made colder or warmer, the change should be very gradual. Persons who have not had experience in transporting fish should always have a thermometer, so that the temperature can be tested. A safe plan is to keep the water a few degrees colder than that in which the fish have been living. In warm weather this can be done by using ice, which, if placed directly in the cans, should be broken in small pieces.

Watch your fish carefully and do not let them suffer. If you cannot give them a change of water, you can refresh them and carry them long distances by re-aerating the water, either by drawing it off into a pail and then pouring it back into the can, or by dipping it from the can and raising it high, allow it to strike on the inverted cover of the can, upon which the fall will be broken, and from thence, it will fall quite gently on the fish.

While the fish are in motion, either on the cars or in a wagon, there is but little danger of losing them because of the jostling about and consequent aeration of the water ; but when they are standing still, careful watch must be kept over them constantly, and those having fish in charge should not sleep, as in that case they would run an almost certain risk of losing them. Large fish show signs of distress by coming to the top of the water, and some kinds, as for instance, trout, will make frantic endeavors to jump out of the can. Young fry at first swim about uneasily, roll their eyes, turn on their sides, and unless relief is given them immediately, they will be dead in a very few minutes.

The number of fish of the bass and perch families,

that can be carried safely in a can of the size mentioned above is from ten to thirty, according to the
size, ranging from one-fourth of a pound to two
pounds, and of the salmon and trout families from
four to six thousand young fry can be carried.
The fry of shad and white fish are much smaller
than the salmon and trout, and, therefore, eight to
ten thousand can be taken in each can. About six
or eight cans are all one person should attempt to
take charge of at one trip, unless the circumstances
are very favorable or he has had experience.

The cultivation of fish should receive the attention of every farmer who has a stream or a pond,
and he should learn the best means of transporting
them.

CHAPTER XXIII.

HOW TO SHIP FISH EGGS.

THE eggs, or spawn, of fish are now shipped to
nearly all parts of the globe, almost as readily as the
seeds of plants or vegetables, but, as they are
"perishable property," there are certain conditions that must be more strictly observed than is
necessary in packing and shipping the seeds of
vegetation. The spawn of certain kinds of fish can
be sent only a short distance, on account of their
rapid development.

The principal points necessary for the successful
shipment of fish eggs on a long journey, are care

and skill in packing them, and also judgment and experience to determine when the eggs are in the proper condition for the trip. The eggs must also be packed so as to maintain as even a temperature as possible, and withstand the jars incident to railway and steamship travel. A few degrees of heat or cold are liable to affect them, and a sudden jar, such, for example, as the dropping of the package, would be almost certain to result in the death of all the eggs.

The temperature of the eggs should remain as near that of the water out of which they were taken as possible. The ova best able to stand transportation are of fish belonging to the salmon family, viz., the salmon, speckled trout, salmon trout or lake trout, land-locked salmon, and the like. The eggs of the white fish also stand transportation well. This ability to stand transportation is chiefly from the fact that they are fall spawning fish and require a long period for hatching. This period varies from seventy to one hundred and thirty-five or one hundred and forty days, according to the temperature of the water ; while the eggs of spring spawning fish, as shad, herring, pike, bass, etc., require only from three to ten days, the temperature of the water also affecting them. The warmer it is, the sooner they hatch.

Probably the best way to pack fish spawn in quantities not exceeding ten thousand, to be sent by express, is in small round tin boxes, in the following manner : The boxes are about three inches wide and two and one-half inches deep. A few small holes are punched in the bottom to let the

water run off. A six quart pan is filled with water
deep enough to barely immerse the box in which
the eggs are to be packed.   The bottom of the box
is then covered with moss, and it is placed in the
pan.   The moss used is such as grows in swamps or
in wet places, as on the stones in a brook or the
timbers of an old dam.   It may be collected and
kept all winter in a damp place in a hatching house.
The moss must be well washed to free it from dirt
and insects, and the green fibres must be cut from
the roots with scissors.   Only the green, soft and
living fibres are used and the rest are thrown away.
This fine moss is once   more washed thoroughly.
A very convenient way is to nail wire netting over
the bottom of an old soap box, cut the moss into
this, and dipping it into water, wash thoroughly.
By lifting the box out of the water the moss is
drained and is ready for use.

The eggs are then taken out of the trough and
counted by means of a graduated glass marked
with a file, so as to indicate five hundred or a thousand, having previously counted the eggs carefully so
as to ascertain where the marks should be made.
When the eggs are measured, pour them into a
ladle small enough for the purpose.   Then sink the
ladle beneath the water in the packing box, and by
gentle tipping it, the eggs will fall to the bottom of
the box on the moss, where they may be spread
evenly with a feather. A layer of prepared moss
must then be lightly laid over the eggs, without taking the box entirely out of the water.   Then another
layer of eggs is placed on top, and so on until the
box is filled.   It is then taken out of water and

allowed to stand a little, so that the water may drain off through the holes in the bottom, and the damp, spongy moss be left, which forms an elastic cushion to protect the eggs from the effects of sudden jolts on the journey, and to supply them with oxygen. When the water is all drained off, the covers are to be placed on the boxes, and tied on with stout string. Great care must be taken not to drop the box in handling it, as it would probably result in the death of all the eggs. I have learned this by experience.

A single box of the above dimensions will hold about five hundred eggs of brook trout. The tin boxes are then packed in sawdust in a pail or box, which should be provided with a handle. The sawdust should cover the boxes for at least an inch, and then, if they are not exposed to a freezing temperature, or a hot fire, and if not roughly handled, they will travel thousands of miles in good condition. I have kept them sixty days in such boxes and hatched them successfully.

Care should be used that none of the eggs touch the sides of the box, and they should not be pressed too tightly. Clean, bright, tin boxes, free from rust, should be used, as eggs coming in contact with iron rust almost invariably die. Trout eggs stand transportation best at about twenty days old. Fish eggs are also shipped successfully in large quantities in wooden crates packed in moss, the eggs being laid on mosquito netting, and also covered with a piece of the same, so as to keep them in place and to facilitate unpacking them. They are also shipped in wooden boxes which are fitted with wooden trays, the under sides of which are covered with Canton flannel tightly stretched. Each tray is about an inch deep, and filled even full with eggs so they will not shake about. A hundred thousand or more can be carried successfully in a box about eighteen inches square, for a journey of several days' duration ; but when shipped in this way, they should always be in the charge of an experienced man, who will see that they are properly handled, and kept in a moderate temperature. One man could take care of a million or more of eggs packed in this manner.

CHAPTER XXIV.

CROSS-BREEDING OF FISH.

ALL farmers know something of the attempts that have been made at crossing the breeds of stock, poultry, etc., and the results. The established methods from which the best results have been obtained were discovered by long years of study and actual experiment. Hybridizing also extends to fruits, vegetables and flowers. It will undoubtedly be interesting to know what has been done in the cross-breeding of fish and the results. The first experiment I ever tried in crossing the breeds of fish was about the year 1869, when I made successful crosses of the white fish and salmon trout, and striped bass and shad. These attempts were kept sight of only so far as to hatch out the fry, and what kind of a fish the combination made consequently remains unknown.

In the year 1877, I made some experiments in crossing the native brook trout with the California salmon, the spawn of the latter having been sent from the Pacific coast, and the fish hatched and reared at the Caledonia hatchery. The result of this experiment was that the fish were nearly all deformed in some way. We kept some of them until they were eight or nine years old. They showed characteristics of both parents, but resembled the salmon rather more in general appearance than the other parent. When they were between three and four years old they began to show indications of spawning. One of the peculiarities discovered was that male fish were either absent or sterile. On attempting to take the spawn from the females artificially, an unexpected difficulty was encountered. To all appearances they had the organs of the brook trout and the eggs of salmon, which are much larger than those of the brook or speckled trout. By the careful use of a knife we took the spawn from the fish, gently pressing the forefinger down the fish's abdomen. There being no milters, we tried to fertilize the eggs thus taken, by using a male brook trout, but without success, as none of the fertilized eggs ever produced fish. The original fish grew well, and when about three and a half years old some of them weighed nearly if not quite two pounds. The cross never amounted to anything practically, but had much interest as an experiment. The salmon used had been hatched and reared entirely in fresh water, and were consequently not in as good condition as those in their natural waters.

The most successful cross I have made, and the one which produced the finest fish, was between brook trout and lake or salmon trout. These fish were mostly beautiful in their markings, very symmetrical in shape, and were perfect hybrids in every way. As with the first mentioned cross, the brook-salmon trout showed marked characteristics of both parents. The spots, though not as brilliant as those of the speckled trout, were much brighter than those of the salmon trout, but in shape they seemed to more nearly resemble the lake trout than the other. They breed naturally, and a fair percentage of their eggs hatch. Their spawning period comes in almost exactly between that of the brook trout and salmon trout, which is from about October 25 to November 25, the straight salmon trout commencing earlier and the brook trout later. The size of the eggs produced by the hybrids was also nearly exactly between those of the respective parent fish. The speckled trout eggs of Caledonia Creek measure six eggs to the inch, while the salmon trout measure four and a half eggs to the inch—the cross coming in between the two, measuring five eggs to the inch.

The hybrid fish have grown to a weight of over five pounds, strong and vigorous fighters on the hook, and equal to either of their parents as table fish. We have also carried this experiment still farther by crossing the hybrids with the straight brook trout, giving us a fish one-fourth salmon trout and three-fourths brook trout, with characteristics proportionate to the cross. We then crossed this fish with the brook trout, which gave us a fish one-eighth salmon trout and seven-eighths brook trout, and these fish can scarcely be told from the straight brook trout, even by an expert.

I have also made other attempts at crossing different breeds of fish with more or less success, but as yet I cannot say that any particular practical benefit has been derived from such attempts. They are valuable in so far as demonstrating what can be done in this direction. In fish culture as well as nearly everything else, all discoveries of value have been the result of actual experiment, and it is through this means that we ascertain the truth or falsity of our theories.